RACE, ECONOMICS, AND APOLOGETICS:
IS THERE A CONNECTION?

Luke Bobo

Copyright © 2019 by Luke B. Bobo

Race, Economics, and Apologetics: Is There a Connection?
by Luke B. Bobo

Publisher: Pursuing the Greater Good, 2019
Printed in the United States of America

ISBN: 978-0-578-46009-3

All rights reserved. No part of this document may be reproduced or transmitted in any form, by any means (electronic, photocopying, recording, or otherwise) without the written permission of the author.

Unless otherwise indicated, Bible quotations are taken from The Holy Bible, English Standard Version. ESV® Text Edition: 2016. Copyright © 2001 by Crossway Bibles, a publishing ministry of Good News Publishers.

Table of Contents

Introduction

Deacon Ralph Johnson moves slowly and laboriously, shuffling as he walks. But ask him about his wife Connie and her ordeal at work, and he beams with pride. Everyone at the General Services Administration Building in Kansas City, Missouri knew Connie was a Christian because of the Bible on her desk and the Christian trinkets adorning her work area. One co-worker constantly harassed and ridiculed Connie as he passed her desk. He would often say, "How can you believe that rubbish?"

Connie believed the implications of Genesis 1:26-28 and treated this co-worker with dignity and respect, just as she treated the rest of her co-workers. With the Spirit's enablement, Connie regularly produced the fruit of the Spirit (Galatians 5:22-23), living a beautifully attractive life at her workplace.

One day the harassing co-worker's wife was involved in a life-threatening car accident. Just after the incident, the co-worker called the office and asked to speak with Connie, who offered to pray for him and his wife. Miraculously, his wife's health improved. Some time later this co-worker approached Connie and said, "I want to give my life to Christ." Shortly thereafter, his wife accepted Christ as her Lord and Savior. Of course, the Holy Spirit was already working in the hearts of this man and his wife. Yet defending the faith or doing apologetics occurs at the intersection of God's sovereignty and human responsibility. So what part did Connie play? She embodied the gospel imperatives. Her life was an apologetic, a defense of what she believed.

The English word "apologetics" derives from the Greek word *apologia*, which means "to give a defense of what one believes." As recorded in 1 Peter 3:14-15,[1] "But even if you should suffer for righteousness' sake, you will be blessed. Have no fear of them, nor be troubled, but in your hearts honor Christ the Lord as holy, always being prepared to make a defense (or an apologetic) to anyone who asks you for a reason for the hope that is in you; yet do it with gentleness and respect." Mark Ryan, director of the Francis Schaeffer Institute at Covenant Theological Seminary, offers the succinct definition for apologia, "to give a word back." In both instances, apologetics is described as a verbal explanation.

I argue that in our post-Christian and highly anti-religious culture, where there is a cacophony of voices, and where, in the words of Pastor Chris Brooks, "The church is struggling with a PR [public relations] problem,"[2] the most impactful apologetic is not a verbal argument at all. In this day and age, the most effective apologetic for both individual Christians and the church as a whole is an embodied apologetic. Jesus'

---

[1] English Standard Version used throughout unless stated otherwise.
[2] Brooks made this remark at the inaugural Stakeholder Forum of Made to Flourish held in June 2018 in Kansas City, Missouri. Brooks is the pastor of Evangel Ministries in Detroit, Michigan.

life was beautifully attractive because it was an apologetic. Furthermore, it is an apologetic worth imitating.

I work at Made to Flourish.[3] Our tagline is a "pastor's network for the common good." At Made to Flourish, we desire to assist pastors in empowering their congregations in the vital integration of faith, work, and economic wisdom. To grow in economic wisdom begins with gaining an understanding of the economy. The economy is a social enterprise. The economy is a "social system through which people organize their work and disperse its fruits. It includes employment and pay, property ownership, exchange, business, and investment."[4] Sadly, not all people have access to this economy. So, we need to ask, "Who has and who does not have unhindered access to the economy?" African-American men still have difficulty gaining access due to "racist attitudes in the workplace,"[5] writes Brooks. Securing unfettered access to the economy for all people—especially for people of color—is a prime opportunity to exercise an embodied apologetic.

The 2015 film *Chi-Raq* adapts the ancient Greek play *Lysistrata* and sets it amid Chicago's gang violence culture. The film uses the phrase "underground economy" to refer to economic life outside the rule of law, i.e., the economy of illegal transactions. The film is an instance of art imitating life, because unfortunately, many African Americans have not been afforded the privilege of unhindered access to the economy. Thus, many have been forced to participate in

---

[3] See Madetoflourish.org.
[4] Self, *Flourishing Churches*, xxiv.
[5] Brooks, "Quiet Death," July 12, 2018.

underground economies. As Matthew Desmond insightfully points out, "High rates of joblessness among black men with little education obscured the fact that many of these men did regularly work, if not in the formal labor market."[6] Desmond is referring to the underground economy that many African-American men are forced to work in because they have been excluded from the *above ground* economy. Yet exclusion comes at a great cost.

Pope Francis expounds on the cost of excluding African Americans and others from the economy, writing, "Until exclusion and inequality in society [and in the economy] and between peoples is reversed, it will be impossible to eliminate violence... When a society – whether local, national or global – is willing to leave a part of itself on the fringes, no political programs or resources spent on law enforcement or surveillance systems can indefinitely guarantee tranquility."[7] The scattered church, I believe, is missing an opportunity for an embodied apologetic to address some of these racial economic disparities and inequalities. The church is divinely and uniquely equipped and empowered to attack and eradicate our racialized economy. But what is a racialized economy?

---

[6] Desmond, *Evicted*, 141.
[7] Francis, *The Joy of the Gospel*, 50-51.

Chapter 1

Racialized Economics

Biologically speaking, whites and blacks are more than 99 percent the same.[8] Biologically speaking, race should not matter; but socially, educationally, politically, and economically, race matters much in our American milieu. As Dr. Shawn L. Alexander, associate professor of African and African-American studies and the director of the Langston Hughes Center, University of Kansas, quips, "Race, biologically *means nothing*, but it means everything." Our lives are undeniably ordered by race, a social construct invented by white human beings. All social institutions, including the economy, are governed by race.

"Race and wealth," writes Hayes-Greene and colleagues, "come together in an intricate Gordian knot."[9] The statement "Economics is racialized,"[10] is an assertion that whites

---

[8] Listen to the *Scene on Radio* Podcast, *Seeing White*.

[9] Hayes-Greene, Plihcik, and Hunter, *Racial Equity Workshop*, Phase 1, 27.

[10] Jeremy Main said this during his opening remarks at Covenant Theological Seminary's City Ministry Initiative (CMI) Conference, "Gentrification and the Church: Moving from Displacement to Beloved Community," on April 13, 2018.

seemingly have unencumbered access to the economy while blacks, historically and even today, struggle to have unhindered access to the economy. In other words, a racialized economy means that the social system is tilted to favor whites over blacks.

We have, for many centuries, lived in an era of racialized economics, and there is a preponderance of evidence that supports this claim. For example, the *Washington Post* reported, "The wealth gap between white and black Americans has more than tripled in the past 50 years, according to Federal Reserve data. The typical black family had zero wealth in 1968. Today the median net worth of white families — $171,000 — is 10 times that of black families."[11]

Simple math tells us that the median net worth of black families hovers around a paltry $17,000. I love math. I first met my future wife at the University of Kansas when I was her math tutor. However, it does not take a math enthusiast to see there is a huge disparity between the median wealth of a black family and a white family. This disparity is a glaring example of the result of racialized economics.[12]

---

[11] Jan, "Report: No Progress," accessed August 28, 2018, http://www.washingtonpost.com/news/wonk/wp/2018/02/26/repor t-no-progress-for-african-americans-on-homeownership-unemployment-and-incarceration-in-50-years/?noredirect=on&utm_term=.860d40553adc.

[12] This median wealth disparity is not far fetched. For example, a five-year estimate (2012-2016), whites earn $52,248 and blacks earn $32,923 in my home state of Missouri; and in our neighboring state, Kansas, whites earn $55,565 and blacks earn $33,887. See American Community Survey, accessed June, 2018, https://factfinder.census.gov/faces/nav/jsf/pages/index.xhtml.

But how did we get here and what are some present-day manifestations of racialized economics? And how can the church embody the gospel or serve as an apologetic?

Chapter 2

How Did We Get Here?

Organizing Conceptual Framework

Racialized economics begins with the formation of an intentional organizing framework. There are many takeaways from the fourteen-part "Seeing White" series on the *Scene on Radio* podcast, but one of the most glaringly obvious takeaways is that our modern society was formed to accommodate and sustain the power and privilege of the white male, and white people in general. Greg Thompson, speaking on the topic of the *Virtues of Leadership*, agrees. Speaking to leaders at the University of Oklahoma, Thompson remarked, "The civic institutions of this country were built for white males for the sake of their thriving."[13]

The Sibley Family established Lindenwood University in St. Charles, Missouri in the 1800s for female students only because white women were not permitted to attend the same colleges as white males. Schools such as Haskell University in Lawrence, Kansas were established because Native Americans were not allowed to attend the same schools as white males. Many historically black colleges and universities

---

[13] Thompson, "Virtues of Leadership," Institute for the Study of Human Flourishing, University of Oklahoma, accessed August 28, 2018, https://www.youtube.com/watch? v=VY6iBsGQddo.

were established because black males were not permitted at colleges attended by white males.

Today, whiteness is an ideology that purports that "whiteness is supreme, better, best,"[14] and this ideology "permeates the air we breathe — in our schools, in our offices, and in our country's common life."[15] Whiteness as a seminal organizing principle finds its origin in the mid-fifteenth century. On August 8, 1444, Zurara, the historian for Prince Henry of Portugal, provided this commentary on the 235 slaves forcibly deported from the port of Lagos (and later divvied up): "And these, placed all together in that field, were a marvelous sight; for amongst them, were some white enough, fair to look upon, and well proportioned; others were less white like mulattoes; others again were as black as Ethiopians, and so ugly, both in features and in body, as almost to appear (to those who saw them) the images of a lower hemisphere."[16] By "lower hemisphere," Christian intellectual Zurara means hell.

Later, author Willie James Jennings recounts what Christopher Columbus reports to Ferdinand and Isabella after completing his third voyage to help them grasp the details of Spain's New World. Columbus reports, "The next day there came from the east a large canoe with 24 men in it, all of them young and bearing weapons… As I said, they were all young and fine looking and *not negroes* but rather the

---

14 Brown, *I'm Still Here*, 22-23.
15 Brown, *I'm Still Here*, 22-23.
16 Jennings, *Christian Imagination*, 18. Also listen to *Scene on Radio* Podcast, *Seeing White*, Part 2.

whitest of all those that I had seen in the Indies, and they were graceful and had fine bodies and long smooth hair cut in the Castilian manner."[17]

The implication or "logic of Columbus' description is obvious — the comparison begins with the known, the self."[18] Another implication of this comparison with the self is that while the "color white did not carry explicit racial connotations, [it] signified culture, refinement and a 'just like us' designation."[19] Most importantly, "Whiteness begins to emerge as the organizing conceptual frame and blackness appears as the fundamental *tool* of that organizing conceptuality."[20] Whiteness became *the standard*; whiteness became synonymous with greater ingenuity, easier to convert, more intelligence, and higher.[21] Blackness became an instrument and synonymous with the opposite, i.e., less ingenuity, harder to convert, less intelligence, and lower.[22]

Contempt for Black Bodies

Contempt for black human beings, and a nascent form of white supremacy, has its beginning in medieval Europe. It was okay to treat black bodies inhumanely, as objects or mere cargo during the Middle Passage or transatlantic slave trade. The traveling accommodations of these black bodies (men, women, and children) on ships crossing the ocean were

---

[17] Jennings, *Christian Imagination*, 29 (*italics* mine).
[18] Jennings, *Christian Imagination*, 30.
[19] Jennings, *Christian Imagination*, 29-30.
[20] Jennings, *Christian Imagination*, 25 (*italics* mine).
[21] Jennings, *Christian Imagination*, 29-30.
[22] Jennings, *Christian Imagination*, 29-30.

horrid and inhumane, to say the least. "One slave might have to sit between the legs of another. Lying down, he might not have space enough to turn over. The height of the space between decks often did not allow him to stand erect, perhaps not even to sit up. Usually each man was shackled either to another man (whose language he might or might not understand) or to a group of men by a long chain that ran through rings on their arms… that meant that, unable to reach tubs and buckets used as toilets, they were forced to relieve themselves where they lay, sat, or stood. Since almost everyone was seasick and had diarrhea or "the blood flux," these lodgings stank unbearably. Candles would not burn in the fetid air."[23]

Joy DeGruy describes their accommodations this way: "Millions were forced onto cargo ships bound for unknown lands that included Brazil, the West Indies, Europe, and the United States, among others. These people were loaded onto ships and crammed together with sometimes less than 18 inches between them. Here they would dwell for many weeks to several months in the bowels of the ship. They were deprived of any human comfort and shared in a collective misery. This disgusting place was where they slept, wept, ate, defecated, urinated, menstruated, vomited, gave birth, and died."[24]

Again, if whiteness is the standard, and if whiteness is superior, then there is no moral violation, no cognitive dissonance in treating blacks as less than human because

---

[23] Schneider and Schneider, *Slavery in America*, 31-32.
[24] DeGruy, *Post Traumatic*, 57.

blackness is inferior or less than whiteness. This contempt for black bodies, as a belief, traveled across the waters to America. Civic, educational, economic, and social institutions were established in America with this reductionist belief about black bodies in mind.

An Organizing Conceptual Framework
Gives Rise to Racism

Whiteness as an organizing conceptual framework blossomed further in America. "Whiteness," explains Lund, "is centered on the relationships between racial categories and power, concentrating on the privileges granted only to whites."[25] Consequently, "racial inequality results from a system of power and exclusion in which whites accumulate economic opportunities and advantages."[26] Blacks, instead of accumulating wealth, dis-accumulate wealth under this white organizational structure. And power, as exercised by the majority culture, maintains this organization of whiteness. That's why Love and Grandpre can write, "Racism is not about being mean; it is about the power that white people have developed through their exploitation of black people and other people of color."[27]

Sadly, this exploitation of black bodies has been institutionalized. The relentless exercise of this power by the majority and the contempt for the black body has given rise to racism. That is why the late Dr. Martin Luther King, Jr.

---

[25] Lund, "The Nature of White Privilege": 16.
[26] Brown, et al., *Whitewashing Race,* 228.
[27] Love and Grandpre, *The Black Book,* vii-viii.

penned the words, "Racism is a philosophy based on a *contempt for life*. It is the arrogant assertion that *one race is the center of value and object of devotion,* before which other races must kneel in submission."[28] This philosophy is not benign. Potter explains the significance of the suffix -ism. The suffix -ism means that "whatever comes in front of the suffix *–ism* is the *center* of reality and the measure of everything."[29]

Think of postmodernism, Hinduism, and humanism. Now, think about the insidious -ism, racism. This means a racialized society such as America is one in which the white race is the center of reality and the measure of everything. This is the prevailing worldview in our country. So then, "Racism involves the ideas (i.e., legitimations) and practices (i.e., discrimination) that create and maintain a white racial privilege which is responsible for both past and present forms of racial inequality."[30] Racism, and all its forms, has led to an uneven playing field for African Americans socially, educationally, and especially, economically.

---

28 King, *Where Do We Go from Here,* 74 (*italics* mine).
29 Potter, 3 *Theories,* 3 (*italics* mine).
30 Thomas, "Anything But Race."

Chapter 3

Wealth Creation for Whites and the Black Body As a Tool

The black body, as the film *Get Out* (2017) so sadly portrayed, is reduced to a *fundamental tool* in a society organized to maintain or preserve whiteness. This is no truer than in America's 265-year-long institution of chattel slavery, the nadir of black body[31] exploitation. Slavery in the United States is a clearly blatant contradiction of the tenet, "all men are created equal… endowed by their Creator with certain unalienable Rights, that among these are Life, Liberty and the Pursuit of Happiness."[32] As Robin Diangelo comments, "The United States was founded on the principle that all people are created equal. Yet the nation began with the attempted genocide of Indigenous people and the theft of their land. [White] American wealth was built on the labor of kidnapped and enslaved Africans and their descendants."[33]

The black person greatly boosted the white slave owner's bottom line because his labor was free. A few slaves, however,

---

[31] Other examples of exploitation of black bodies include the Tuskegee Syphilis Experiment, 1932-1972; also see Rebecca Skloot's book, *The Immortal Life of Henrietta Lacks* (2011).

[32] Second paragraph of the United States Declaration of Independence.

[33] Diangelo, *White Frailty*, xiii.

could participate in the economy but there were strings attached. While "legally, slaves could own nothing, some earned a little money for themselves."[34] Benevolent "plantation owners often *permitted* their slaves to farm small plots and sell their produce or make baskets or brooms for sale; in gray-market transactions, slaves sold 'moonshine' and stolen goods."[35] Sometimes slaves were permitted to "hire out" themselves. When their owners did not need their services, slaves were sometimes permitted to lease their labor to someone else. Under this arrangement, a slave also promised to pay his owner a profit out of the wages he earned by running his business or working for another employer.

Many slaves, like Frederick Douglass[36] and Charles White,[37] were able to buy their emancipation by paying their masters their monetized value (in dollars). However, a slave's master might suddenly and capriciously rescind a slave's opportunity to hire himself out or to farm a small plot of land. Clearly, under this racial caste system, the black body was a dispensable commodity and at the whim of the slave owner. As a commodity, the black body could be auctioned, traded, bought, and sold. Our Supreme Court upheld the idea that blacks were mere property through the nineteenth century. As Rausch has written, "The Supreme Court ruled in 1857 that Dred and Harriet Scott, despite having lived in free territories,

---

[34] Schneider and Schneider, *Slavery in America*, 62.
[35] Schneider and Schneider, *Slavery in America*, 62 (*italics* mine).
[36] Schneider and Schneider, *Slavery in America*, 63.
[37] Stampp, *The Peculiar Institution*, 96-97.

were nonetheless slaves and therefore *property* with no right to sue."[38]

Imagine the trauma inflicted on blacks when husbands, wives, and children were ripped apart from each other. Epigeneticists are now asserting that the historical and daily trauma African Americans experience is passed on to generations, even to the fetus in utero. Christopher W. Kuzawa and Elizabeth Sweet conclude that, "There is extensive evidence for a social origin to prematurity and low birth weight in African Americans, reflecting pathways such as the effects of discrimination on maternal stress physiology. In light of the inverse relationship between birth weight and adult cardiovascular disease (CVD), there is now a strong rationale to consider developmental and epigenetic mechanisms as links between early life environmental factors like maternal stress during pregnancy and adult race-based health disparities in diseases like hypertension, diabetes, stroke, and coronary heart disease."[39]

Trauma of this magnitude and the generational effects transcend cultures. For instance, Kellerman studied the trauma passed on, genetically, to Holocaust survivors and their descendants.[40] The title of his paper asks, "Epigenetic transmission of Holocaust trauma: can nightmares be inherited?" The research unequivocally answers in the affirmative. So, is it also possible that slavery trauma has been passed on to other generations? DeGruy answers that question

---

[38] Rausch, "On a Civil Rights Trail" (*italics* mine).
[39] Kuzawa and Sweet, "Epigenetics and the embodiment of race."
[40] Kellermann, "Epigenetic transmission of Holocaust trauma."

with the title of her book, *Post Traumatic Slave Syndrome*. Multigenerational trauma resulting from centuries of slavery, oppression, institutional racism, and modern microaggressions is indisputable and explains why whites are uninformed when they suggest blacks "Just get over it."

DeGruy reminds us, "During the time of American chattel slavery, it was exceedingly rare for a slave to be freed and rarer still for an enslaved person to buy his or her freedom."[41] When slaves were freed after the Civil War, "Many states decreed that blacks had to work for any wages the [Southern plantation] owners deemed fair."[42] This law is one of many Black Codes introduced in 1865 to control the movement and activities of those recently freed. Other codes "set out what work blacks were allowed to do, where they could do it, and what hours they could work. The codes prevented blacks from owning land, voting, suing, and sitting on juries."[43] Within a few years the federal courts ruled these codes were too harsh and overturned them, but whites did not sit by idly and let blacks prosper.

Consider the Jim Crow era. The Jim Crow "separate but equal" dogma and practice enforced racial segregation in the South between the end of Reconstruction in 1877 and the beginning of the civil rights movement in the 1950s. There were Jim Crow schools, Jim Crow restaurants, and Jim Crow water fountains. Life during Jim Crow did not give blacks a

---

[41] DeGruy, *Post Traumatic*, 34.
[42] DeGruy, *Post Traumatic*, 64.
[43] DeGruy, *Post Traumatic*, 64.

leg up on earning wealth. Rather, practices such as convict leasing put black wealth earning further and further behind.

During this period — after slavery ended — African Americans were arbitrarily arrested. Consequently, many of them were hit with court costs and fines they could not pay. To pay off these exorbitant debts, "prisoners were *sold* as forced laborers to lumber camps, brickyards, railroads, farms, plantations, and dozens of corporations throughout the South."[44] In the South, this practice "disenfranchised blacks and discriminated against them in virtually every sphere of life, lending sanction to a racial ostracism that extended to schools, churches, housing, jobs, restrooms, hotels, restaurants, hospitals, orphanages, prisons, funeral homes, morgues, and cemeteries."[45]

Imagine if educational opportunities had been equal for blacks and whites. Carruthers and Wanamaker explain what could have been: "Education equality would have been a powerful tool for raising black economic standing in the South; [but] the lost opportunity reduced the earnings capacity of this generation of black southerners by up to 50 percent."[46] Gillian B. White further illuminates the consequence of the separate but equal doctrine and practice, noting that "The explicit sanctioning of segregation by Jim Crow meant that black public schools lacked resources and public funding — shortcomings that limited the skill sets and

---

[44] Alexander, *New Jim Crow*, 31 (*italics* mine).
[45] Alexander, *New Jim Crow*, 35.
[46] Carruthers and Wannmaker, "Separate and Unequal in the Labor Market."

education levels of young, black men during this period, which in turn limited their job opportunities."[47]

In sum, survivors of Jim Crow suffered real existential harm, including economic harm, all of which help us to contextualize both their trauma and struggles with agency today.[48] For many blacks, "Life, Liberty, and the Pursuit of Happiness" is still a dream deferred or abandoned.

---

[47] White, "Searching for the Origins of the Racial Wage Disparity in Jim Crow America."
[48] Bradley, "Finally Healing the Words of Jim Crow."

Chapter 4

Racialized Economics: Present-Day Examples

The brutal, oppressive institution of slavery in the United States made many whites extremely wealthy. Blacks, on the other hand, did not fare so well due to a racialized economic system. Our racialized economic system continues today because racist attitudes and practices are woven into its very fabric. Racist attitudes are in the DNA of our economic system. Consider three manifestations of our racialized economy: housing discrimination and segregation, hiring discrimination and lack of upward mobility, and mass incarceration of black men.

Housing Discrimination and Segregation. Most Americans know that one can accumulate wealth by investing in real estate. For African Americans, buying real estate has been easier said than done because of a practice known as redlining. The practice of redlining was outlawed in the 1970s; however, redlining continues today de facto. Janelle O'Dea reports that, "Nearly 50 years after the federal Fair Housing Act was signed into law, banning racial discrimination in lending, black prospective homebuyers in the St. Louis area continue to be denied conventional mortgage loans at a much higher rate than whites—even when controlling for income, loan amount and neighborhood. In the metropolitan area, African Americans who apply for conventional mortgage loans are 2.5 times more likely to be denied than non-Hispanic whites."[49]

What is redlining? As the word suggests, with the help of realtors, bankers drew a red line around certain neighborhoods. Homeowners in those neighborhoods, often African Americans, were denied loans to refurbish or invest in their homes. As a result, their houses depreciated in value. Instead of accruing wealth through appreciation of their property value, African American homeowners lost wealth.

What is the origin of redlining? In 1933, to rescue households that were about to default, Franklin D. Roosevelt's administration created the Home Owners' Loan Corporation (HOLC). According the Rothstein, "HOLC mortgages had low interest rates, but the borrowers still were obligated to make regular payments. To assess risk, the HOLC wanted to know something about the condition of the house and of surrounding houses in the neighborhood to see whether the property would likely maintain its value. So, the HOLC hired local real estate agents to make the appraisals on which refinancing decisions could be based."[50]

Not surprising, these agents considered the racial makeup of the neighborhoods in gauging risk. Rothstein continues, "The HOLC created color-coded maps of every metropolitan area

---

[49] O'Dea, "Lending discrimination, redlining still plague St. Louis."
[50] Rothstein, *The Color of Law*, 64.

in the nation, with the safest neighborhoods colored green and the riskiest colored red. A neighborhood earned a red color if African Americans lived in it, even if it was a solid middle-class neighborhood of single-family homes."[51]

Home ownership and investment in home property is how many whites amassed their wealth, but because of private discrimination and public policy, African Americans' residential options were severely constrained. Gordon once again shines the spotlight on the city of St. Louis, noting that "Throughout the twentieth century, private discrimination and public policy combined — intentionally and explicitly — to constrain the residential options available to African Americans, to confine them to certain wards or neighborhoods, and to stem what was widely perceived (in St. Louis and elsewhere) as the threat of invasion posed by north-to-south and rural-to-urban migration."[52] Note the phrase "and elsewhere." These practices (e.g., racial zoning and state-enforced restrictive deed covenants) and policies were replicated and enforced in other American cities. Economics is racialized, and it is not a local phenomenon.

Hiring Discrimination and Lack of Upward Mobility. I know a dear sister named Shanquita. She is bright and funny. Shanquita is a not a white-sounding name. Based on the research[53] of Marianne Bertrand and Sendhil Mullainathan at the University of Chicago and the Massachusetts Institute of

---

[51] Rothstein, *The Color of Law*, 64.
[52] Gordon, *Mapping Decline*, 11.
[53] Bertrand and Mullainathan, "Are Emily and Greg More Employable than Lakisha and Jamal?"

Technology, the odds of Shanquita receiving a callback for a job interview are highly unlikely. Bertrand and Mullainathan wanted to measure racial discrimination in the labor market. They mailed résumés in response to the help-wanted sections in Chicago and Boston newspapers. Half of the résumés had African-American-sounding names, and half had white-sounding names. All the other information, including educational background, work history, etc., was identical. The researchers also sent out résumés with differing names and different levels of work experience. In all, they sent out 5,000 résumés for a variety of positions, from clerical to sales managers.

The results were illuminating. Résumés with white-sounding names received 50 percent more callbacks than black names. Furthermore, "white names with high-quality work experience received 30 percent more callbacks than white names with low-quality experience. However, black names with high-quality work experience received no more callbacks than black names with low-quality work experience."[54]

Researchers Darolia, Koedel, Martorell, Wilson, and Perez-Arce flipped the script and conducted another field experiment. Instead of selecting first names that were suggestive of race, they chose last names suggestive of race for black, Hispanic, and white applicants. Positively, they found "little evidence to suggest that employers discriminate by race or gender in responding to résumés from job

---

[54] DeGruy, *Post Traumatic*, 80.

applications. One explanation for our findings is that we selected names for résumés to indicate race and gender without further indications of socioeconomic status."[55]

What is key here is the phrase "socioeconomic status." The implication is that employers read some first names, such as Jamal or Shanquita, as low socioeconomic status, while black-sounding last names such as Washington and Jefferson do not suggest low socioeconomic status. What is in a name? Apparently, these two studies suggest employers see much in a person's first and last name.[56] Hiring employers' antennas are attuned to detect first and last names that suggest a low socioeconomic standing.

Even when blacks cross the threshold into companies, they have fewer opportunities for upward mobility and access to power than their white peers.[57] Look at your company: who sits at the top? Consider the "racial breakdown of the people who control our institutions in 2016-2017"[58]:

---

[55] Darolia et al., "Race and Gender Effects."
[56] See Benjamin Norquist essay, *Race-Based Hiring Disparities as a Theological Problem*, on the Faith at Work Summit 2018 website, for more on this topic.
[57] Thomas, "Anything But Race."
[58] Diangelo, *White Fragility*, 31.

United States Congress:	90 percent white
Top military advisors:	100 percent white
United States governors:	96 percent white
People who decide which news is covered:	85 percent white
People who decide which music is produced:	95 percent white
Teachers:	82 percent white
Owners of men'sprofessional football teams:	97 percent white

Clearly, from this partial list, whites dominate what Diangelo calls a "sociopolitical economic system."[59] "This system of structural power," writes Diangelo, "privileges, centralizes, and elevates white people as a group."[60] This grip on power and control by whites means that the white life experience remains normative.

Mass Incarceration. "Today," writes Bryan Stevenson, "we [the United States of America] have the highest rate of

---

[59] Diangelo, *White Fragility*, 30.
[60] Diangelo, *White Fragility*, 30.

incarceration rate in the world."[61] And "one in every three black male babies born in this century is expected to be incarcerated."[62] During a TED Talk, Stevenson added more specificity, stating that "one out of three African-American men, ages 18 to 30, is in jail, in prison, on probation or on parole."[63] Former Illinois capital punishment lawyer, Scott Turow, asserts in *Ultimate Punishment: A Lawyer's Reflections on Dealing with the Death Penalty*, that a white life is more valuable than a black life in the criminal justice system. In other words, a white defendant who perpetrated a crime against a black person will get a lighter sentence. On the other hand, a black defendant who perpetrated a crime against a white person will likely get a harsher sentence. Perhaps this phenomenon explains the disproportionate number of African Americans in prison.

Race isn't the only factor; so is one's socioeconomic status. Stevenson states, "We have to reform a system of criminal justice that continues to treat people better if they are rich and guilty than if they are poor and innocent."[64] There is racial bias and discrimination against the poor in the criminal justice system. Our criminal justice system takes potential wage owners and family providers off the streets for minor, nonviolent crimes. As Desmond explains, incarcerating black men also impacts black women and their children: "If incarceration had come to define the lives of men from

---

[61] Stevenson, *Just Mercy*, 15.
[62] Stevenson, *Just Mercy*, 15.
[63] Stevenson, "We Need to Talk about Justice," accessed August 28, 2018, https://www.ted.com/talks/bryan_stevenson_we need_to_talk_about_an_injustice.
[64] Stevenson, *Just Mercy*, 313.

impoverished black neighborhoods, eviction was shaping the lives of women. Poor black men were locked up. Poor black women were locked out."[65]

With more black men being locked up, black mothers often struggle to make monthly ends meet. More black men locked up disadvantages black women, but advantages white men. With more black men locked up, white people's access to jobs is unobstructed. The mass incarceration of African American men works, quips Butler, "like an employment stimulus plan for working class white people, who don't have to compete for jobs with all the black men who are locked up, or who are underground because they have outstanding arrest warrants, or who have criminal records that make obtaining legal employment exceedingly difficult."[66]

Stevenson founded the Equal Justice Initiative,[67] "a legal practice dedicated to defending the poor, the wrongly condemned, and those trapped in the furthest reaches of our criminal justice system."[68] Adding further harm to the wrongfully condemned, most people released from prison after being proven innocent receive no money, no assistance, and no counseling from the state that wrongly imprisoned them. Although the number of states that provide compensation has increased, "almost half of all states

---

[65] Desmond, *Evicted*, 98.

[66] Butler, "The Chokehold," 17.

[67] See website https://eji.org/.

[68] Taken from the back cover of *Just Mercy: A Story of Justice and Redemption*.

(twenty-two) offer no compensation to the wrongly imprisoned."[69]

To add insult to injury, "while other states have caps of more than a million dollars, and many have no cap at all, several states impose onerous eligibility requirements. In some jurisdictions, if the person lacks the support of the prosecuting attorney who wrongly convicted him, compensation is denied."[70] Seeking reparations for the wrongly accused, imprisoned, and condemned seems to be an obvious goal for those who embody the gospel.

Just Think

Take a moment to ponder these instances of racialized economics. Think about the divestiture of businesses or the loss of industries (and jobs) in urban neighborhoods. Think about the dysfunction of the black family. Think about being "constantly suspected, accused, watched, doubted, distrusted, presumed guilty, and even feared."[71] As you ponder, you might begin to see why many African Americans in the inner city suffer from nihilism[72] or profound hopelessness. You might also begin to understand why it may *appear as though* black men are walking around lazily and aimlessly. Many are walking around because they have been locked out of opportunities due to racialized economics.

---

[69] Stevenson, *Just Mercy*, 245.
[70] Stevenson, *Just Mercy*, 245.
[71] Stevenson, *Just Mercy*, 301.
[72] Ellis, *The Rise of Ghetto Nihilism*.

Racialized economics continues today because it is systemic. Yet the church is uniquely and divinely equipped to smash our racialized economic system.

Chapter 5

Embodying the Gospel: Opportunities for the Church

Embodying the gospel is the apologetic needed for our time. Below are six ways the scattered church can embody or put on the gospel in defense of the gospel.

1. *Love.* We must embody love for our neighbor. Jesus summed up the Old Testament laws this way, "Love God with all your heart, with all your soul, with all your mind, and with all your strength. And the second is like it, Love your neighbor as yourself" (Matthew 22:36-40). Jesus teaches in the parable of the Good Samaritan (Luke 10) that all persons, regardless of country of origin, sexual orientation, socioeconomic status, or race are our neighbors. The Good Samaritan "put on love" (Colossians 3:14). Loving our neighbor begins with coming close and listening to our neighbor. Listening precedes responding.

    Practice Renee Watson's mantra, "Great poets listen to their world and respond back."[73] Listen to our neighbor and listen to our world; after listening,

---

[73] Watson, "Five Years After the Levees Broke."

respond back. God wants us to cultivate a hearty and genuine love for our neighbor. This love is not static, complacent, or indifferent. Rather, this love "refuses to see systems and structures of injustice."[74] This love "is troubled by injustice."[75] We love our neighbor by caring for our neighbor. This love seeks to help those who are struggling financially. It is true that money does not buy happiness, but "it helps lift some of the psychological pressures of poverty."[76] Loving others is moving them toward shalom.

Mrs. Pomelia Guyton, my late Sunday school teacher at Friendship Missionary Baptist Church in Kansas City, Missouri, was fond of saying, "People don't care how much you know until they know how much you care." For the purposes of our discussion, let me modify that idiom a bit. "People don't care to hear what we believe until they know how much we care."

2. *Justice.* We must embody justice. Justice is a core gospel principle. Justice and the gospel are inextricably tied together. Doing justice is not like options on a multiple-choice test. Justice matters to God; it is not optional. See Deut. 16:20; Isa. 1:17, 30:18-19, 61:8-9; Amos 5:18-24; Zech. 7:9; Hosea 12:6; Mic. 6:8; Ps. 33:5, 99:4; Matt. 23:23 for proof. If justice matters to God, it should matter to us. Justice is righting wrongs and rendering what is due to a person. Is there a connection

---

[74] Brown, *I'm Still Here,* 176.
[75] Brown, *I'm Still Here,* 176.
[76] Gershon, "Happy, Healthy Economy."

between love and justice? Yes, for "love and justice are the same, for justice is love distributed."[77]

Justice demands action. We are responsible to act justly once we see, learn, and hear of injustice.[78] Bryan Stevenson is more forceful, "We are all implicated when we allow other people to be mistreated. An absence of compassion can corrupt the decency of a community, a state, a nation. Fear and anger can make us vindictive and abusive, unjust, and unfair, until we all suffer from the absence of mercy and we condemn others as much as we victimize others."[79]

We must not only be citizens who see, learn, and hear, but Christian citizens who actively seek justice on behalf of those who cannot. We must seek ways to give all persons equal access to earning a living. We image God when we do justice because God does justice (Gen. 1:26-28; Eph. 5:1). Those bent toward justice realize that, "To become [a] just [society], a society must bring into community all its weak and defenseless ones, its marginal ones, giving them voice and a fair share in the goods of the community."[80]

Justice means speaking up when we see black bodies abused, denied, harassed, and exploited. Justice "means addressing structures of discrimination and

---

[77] *New Dictionary of Christian Ethics & Pastoral Theology*, 13.
[78] Garber, *Visions of Vocation*, 112-135.
[79] Stevenson, *Just Mercy*, 18.
[80] *New Dictionary of Christian Ethics & Pastoral Theology*, 18.

oppression and creating conditions in which all may flourish."[81] Perhaps, that means fighting for restitution for those who experienced lost earnings while they were unjustly locked up. Justice has economic inclusion as one of its goals.

3. *Repentance.* We must embody repentance (and behavior in keeping with repentance). In chapter three of Luke, John the Baptist, the Messiah's herald, preaches to the crowd, "Produce fruit consistent with repentance" (vs. 8). Many ask about the implications of this statement. The crowds ask, "What then should we do?" John replies, "The one who has two shirts must share with someone who has none, and the one who has food must do the same."

Embodying repentance means generosity. The tax collectors ask, "Teacher, what should we do?" John replies, "Don't collect any more than what you have been authorized." Embodying repentance means not cheating others out of their funds, and it means not defrauding our neighbor. Embodying repentance means speaking out against fraudulent abuse. Finally, some soldiers ask, "What should we do?" John answers, "Don't take money from anyone by force or false accusation and be satisfied with your wages." Embodying repentance is a call for contentment and a refusal to be an accomplice in taking someone's money.

---

[81] Toly, *Cities of Tomorrow*, 48.

4. *Serve*. We must embody service. Jesus came to serve and not to be served (Mark 10). To serve well, we must know well. We must read non-white history. We must come close to non-whites and hear their stories. We must, in the words of my friend Denis Haack, give people the "gift of unhurried time." As we come close and as we learn, we will discover that the same institutions that whites benefit from every day have been and continue to be oppressive to blacks. In other words, to serve well and for the common good, we must understand a robust definition of reconciliation as offered by Brenda Salter McNeil who describes it as, "an ongoing spiritual process involving forgiveness, repentance, and justice that restores broken relationships and systems [institutions] to reflect God's original intention for all creation to flourish."[82]

One such broken institution is the educational system. For example, there is a college graduation gap between low-income students and their wealthier peers. Specifically, "there is a disproportionate number of low-income students [who] will no longer be in college by the time the rest of their classmates earn their diplomas."[83] However, "college graduation is essential to economic mobility."[84] How might we, the church, help the hobbled educational system to give low-income students a hope to see college? Alternatively,

[82] McNeil, *Roadmap to Reconciliation*, 22.
[83] Gerson, Summers, and Thompson, *Unleashing Opportunity*, 83.
[84] Gerson, Summers, and Thompson, *Unleashing Opportunity*, 81.

how might we use our privileges or connections to help a low-income kid enter a trade school, not because he or she is not smart; rather, because he or she has proven to be nimble with tools?

Active engagement in the messy and mysterious work of reconciliation is one of the tributaries that places us on the pathway to human flourishing for all. Active engagement in the messy and mysterious work of reconciliation is one of the ways we can collectively put African Americans on the pathway to human flourishing, and specifically to economic flourishing.

5. *Biblical anthropology.* We must embody a biblical anthropology, beginning with this gnomic truth: all persons are imago Dei bearers, and consequently, all persons deserve to be treated with dignity and respect. This means that to treat others as subhuman is to act subhuman. To embody a biblical anthropology means speaking out against subhuman treatment of fellow imago Dei bearers, such as in discriminatory hiring and housing practices. Embodying a biblical anthropology means resisting capitalism's gravitational pull to be transformed from homo imago Dei into a *homo economicus* — an autonomous, individualistic, purely self-interested, materialistic creature.[85]

---

[85] Fikkert and Rhodes, "Homo Economicus Versus Homo Imago Dei," 102.

Those who embody a biblical anthropology are driven not to be autonomous, individualistic, and purely self-interested, but rather communal and interested in the whole of the human race. God intended every person to flourish, as implied in the cultural mandate in Genesis 1:26-28. Adam and Eve were to move across the land, develop culture, and rule righteously for the flourishing of all human beings. We can catapult a person's dignity by helping him or her find employment because humans image God when they work. There is dignity in work because we are introduced to a God who works in the first two chapters of Genesis. Work is intrinsically good, and all work contributes to the common good of all mankind.

6. *Shalom and flourishing.* We must embody shalom and flourishing. One speaker described shalom as "nothing is missing, nothing is broken." Cornelius Plantinga offers a definition of shalom in which the "universal flourishing, wholeness, and delight—a rich state of affairs in which natural needs are satisfied and natural gifts fruitfully employed… Shalom, in other words, is the way things ought to be."[86] We must understand that our flourishing depends on the flourishing of others, and the flourishing of others depends on our flourishing.

   Esther and Mordecai act for the sake of flourishing for the entire city of Susa because they will flourish (see

---

[86] Plantinga, *Not the Way It's Supposed to Be,* 10.

the book of Esther). Jeremiah 29:7 says, "When the city thrives, you will thrive."[87] Flourishing involves mutuality. As Dr. King pointed out, "We are caught in an inescapable network of mutuality, tied in a single garment of destiny."[88] We flourish when all men flourish, especially, the most vulnerable among us.

7. *Ecclesial identity.* We must embody our proper identity as the universal church. The church has a catholic, communal personality. One implication of that reality is that "no church in a given culture may isolate itself from other churches in other cultures declaring itself sufficient to itself and to its own culture. Every church must be open to all other churches."[89] We belong to each other; we are part of one covenant family. We are all — black and white — children of God our Father.

Lastly, God calls and equips the church for the sake of human flourishing. That is exactly why, "the church is not the church if it does not stand for justice."[90] A church not active in pursuing justice undermines its identity.

---

[87] See also Acts 2:44-46; 4:32-37; 2 Cor. 8:9-15; Eph. 4:28; Rom. 12:17-21.
[88] Washington, *Essential Writings and Speeches of Martin Luther King Jr.,* 290.
[89] Volf, *Exclusion and Embrace,* 51.
[90] *Twelve Elements of Economic Wisdom,* 11.

Conclusion

I am greatly encouraged by the news that the proportion of "black men in poverty has fallen from 41% in 1960 to 18% today. More importantly, the share of black men in the middle or upper class—as measured by their family income—has risen from 38% in 1960 to 57% today. In other words, about one in two black men in America has reached the middle class or higher."[91]

Reaching the coveted middle class and reducing racial disparity was achieved in part because of these men's participation in military duty, marriage and family, and the church. On the other hand, I am sobered by Raj Chetty's work, which finds that, "White boys who grew up in rich households are likely to remain that way. Black boys who are also raised at the top are more likely to become poor, instead of staying wealthy in their own adult households. Black boys fare worse than white boys in 99 percent of America, even when children grow up next to each other, with parents who

---

[91] Wilcox, Wang, and Mincy. "Black Men," accessed August 28, 2018, http://www.phillytrib.com/news/black-men-are-succeeding-in-america/article_71a67c96-7f07-11e8-a1ce-.03d67de5efac.html?utm_medium=social&utm_source=facebook&utm_campaign=user-share.

earn similar incomes."[92] More analysis needs to be done to see if these reports can be reconciled; however, two things are certain: we do not live in a post-racial milieu and we have not yet arrived.

More work toward economic justice and shalom needs to be done. Hiring discrimination, residential segregation, and discriminatory mass incarceration of African-American men are pressing issues of our day that have economic implications. We must embody the gospel to address these issues. Embodying the gospel is our apologetic. Our work persists until whiteness as an organizational framework is reorganized or abandoned for the sake of the flourishing of all human beings. Our work continues until diversity and inclusion professionals are no longer required; until we see more non-white men and women heading Fortune 100 and 500 companies; and until we see more non-whites chairing and serving on the boards of these same Fortune 100 and 500 companies.

Our work continues until we restore African Americans' "economic dignity"[93] and dismantle institutions such as predatory payday loan businesses that routinely rape them of their dignity. Our work continues until we can help African Americans recoup lost wealth. In a time when the gospel is

---

[92] PBS, "Black men face economic disadvantages," accessed August 28, 2018, https://www.pbs.org/newshour/show/black-men-face-economic-disadvantages-even-if-they-start-out-in-wealthier-households-new-study-shows.

[93] Gerson, Summers, and Thompson, *Unleashing Opportunity*, 111.

implausible, an embodied, nonverbal, lived apologetic is what is desperately needed in these troubled times.

Bibliography

Alexander, Michelle. *The New Jim Crow: Mass Incarceration in the Age of Colorblindness*. New York: The New Press, 2012.

Bertrand, Marianne, and Mullainathan, Sendhil. "Are Emily and Greg More Employable than Lakisha and Jamal? A Field Experiment on Labor Market Discrimination." University of Chicago Graduate School of Business, National Bureau of Economic Research, July 2003.

Bradley, Anthony. "Finally Healing the Words of Jim Crow: Maybe what we need is transitional justice." *Fathom Magazine*, July 11, 2018.

Brooks, David. "The Quiet Death of Racial Progress." *The New York Times*, July 12, 2018.

Brown, Austin Channing. *I'm Still Here: Black Dignity in A World Made for Whiteness*. New York: Convergent, 2018.

Brown, Michael, Carnoy, Martin, Currie, Elliott, Duster, Troy, Oppenheimer, David B., Schultz, Marjorie M., and Wellman, David. *Whitewashing Race: The Myth of a Color-Blind Society*. Berkeley: University of California Press, 2003.

Butler, Paul. "The Chokehold." *The Crisis Magazine*, Fall 2017.

Carruthers, Celeste K., and Wannmaker, Marianne H. "Separate and Unequal in the Labor Market: Human Capital and the Jim Crow Wage Gap." National Bureau of Economic Research, Working Paper 21947, 2016.

Darolia, Rajeev, Koedel, Cory, Martorell, Paco, Wilson, Katie, and Perez-Arce, Francisco. "Race and Gender Effects on Employer Interest in Job Applicants: New Evidence from a Resume Field Experiment." Spencer Foundation, the Economic and Policy Analysis Research Center at the University of Missouri, August 2015.

DeGruy, Joy. *Post Traumatic Slave Syndrome: America's Legacy of Enduring Injury and Healing*. Portland: Uptone Press, 2017.

Desmond, Matthew. *Evicted: Poverty and Profit in the American City*. New York: Crown Publishers, 2016.

Diangelo, Robin. *White Fragility: Why It's So Hard For White People To Talk About Racism*. Boston: Beacon Press, 2018.

Ellis, Jr., Carl F. "The Rise of Ghetto Nihilism." Unpublished.

Fikkert, Brian, and Rhodes, Michael. "Homo Economicus Versus Homo Imago Dei." *Journal of Markets & Morality* 20, no. 1 (2017).

Francis, Pope. *The Joy of the Gospel*. Frederick, MD: The Word Among Us, 2013.

Garber, Steve. *Vision of Vocation: Common Grace for the Common Good*. Downers Grove, IL: InterVarsity, 2014.

Gershon, Livia. "Happy, Healthy Economy." Accessed August 28, 2018. https://longreads.com/2018/08/06/happy-healthy-economy/.

Gerson, Michael, Summers, Stephanie, and Thompson, Katie. *Unleashing Opportunity: Why Escaping Poverty Requires a Shared Vision of Justice.* Beaver Falls: Falls City Press, 2015.

Gordon, Colin. *Mapping Decline: St. Louis and the Fate of the American City.* Philadelphia, University of Pennsylvania, 2008.

Hayes-Greene, Deena, Plihcik, Suzanne, and Hunter, Wanda. *Racial Equity Workshop, Phase 1: Foundations in Historical and Institutional Racism.* Racial Equity Institute (REI), May 27, 2018.

Jan, Tracy. "Report: No progress for African Americans on homeownership, unemployment and incarceration in 50 years." Accessed August 28, 2018. http://www.washingtonpost.com/news/wonk/wp/2018/02/26/report-no-progress-for-african-americans-on-homeownership-unemployment-and-incarceration-in-50-years/?noredirect=on&utm_term=.860d40553adc.

Jennings, Willie James. *The Christian Imagination: Theology and The Origins of Race.* New Haven: Yale University, 2010.

Kellermann, NP. "Epigenetic transmission of Holocaust trauma: Can nightmares be inherited? Israel Journal of Psychiatry and Related Sciences 50, no. 1, (2013).

King, Jr., Martin Luther. *Where Do We Go From Here: Chaos or Community?* Boston: Beacon Press, 2010.

Kuzawa, Christopher W., and Sweet, Elizabeth. "Epigenetics and the embodiment of race: Developmental origins of US racial disparities in cardiovascular health." American Journal of Human Biology 21, no. 1, (2009).

Love, Dayvon, and Grandpre, Lawrence. *The Black Book: Reflections from the Baltimore Grassroots.* Baltimore: Leaders of a Beautiful Struggle, 2014.

Lund, Carole L. "The Nature of White Privilege in the Teaching and Training of Adults." *New Directions for Adult and Continuing Education.* 125, (2010).

McNeil, Brenda Salter. *Roadmap to Reconciliation: Moving Communities into Unity, Wholeness and Justice.* Downers Grove: InterVarsity, 2015.

O'Dea, Janelle. "Lending discrimination, redlining still plague St. Louis, new data show." Accessed August 28, 2018. https://www.stltoday.com/news/multimedia/special/lending-discrimination-redlining-still-plague-st-louis-new-data-show/article_3e1a6847-799b-58d7-a680-651a0c1a2ea8.html.

PBS. "Black men face economic disadvantages even if they start out in wealthier households, new study shows." Accessed August 28, 2018. https://www.pbs.org/newshour/show/black-men-face-economic-disadvantages-even-if-they-start-out-in-wealthier-households-new-study-shows.

Plantinga, Cornelius. *Not the Way It's Supposed To Be: A Breviary of Sin.* Grand Rapids: Eerdmans, 1995.

Potter, Ellis. *3 Theories of Everything*. Huemoz, Switzerland: Destinée Media, 2012.

Rausch, Robert. "On a Civil Right Trail, Essential Sites and Indelible Detours." *The New York Times*. Accessed August 29, 2018. https://www.nytimes.com/2018/08/06/travel/ civil-rights-trail.html.

Rothstein, Richard. *The Color of Law: A Forgotten History of How Our Government Segregated America*. New York: Liveright, 2017.

Schneider, Dorothy, and Schneider, Carl J. *Slavery in America: From Colonial Times to the Civil War*. New York: Checkmark Books, 2001.

Self, Charlie. *Flourishing Churches and Communities*. Grand Rapids: Christian's Library Press, 2013.

Stampp, Kenneth M. *The Peculiar Institution: Slavery in the Ante-Bellum South*. New York: Vintage Books, 1989.

Stevenson, Bryan. *Just Mercy: A Story of Justice and Redemption*. New York: Spiegel & Grau, 2015.

Stevenson, Bryan. "We Need to Talk About Justice." TED Talk. Accessed August 28, 2018. https://www.ted.com/talks/ bryan_stevenson_we_need_to_talk_about_an_injustice.

Thomas, Melvin. *Anything But Race: The Social Science Retreat From Racism*. North Carolina State University. Accessed August 28, 2018. http://citeseerx.ist.psu.edu/viewdoc/ download?doi=10.1.1.458.4107&rep=rep1&type=pdf.

Thompson, Greg. "Virtues of Leadership." Institute for the Study of Human Flourishing. University of Oklahoma. Accessed August 28, 2018. https://www.youtube.com/watch?v=VY6iBsGQddo.

Toly, Noah J. *Cities of Tomorrow and The City to Come*. Grand Rapids: Zondervan, 2015.

Twelve Elements of Economic Wisdom. Accessed August 29, 2018. https://oikonomianetwork.org/wp-content/uploads/2017/05/TwelveElementsEconomicWisdom8.pdf.

Volf, Miroslav. *Exclusion and Embrace: A Theological Exploration of Identity, Otherness, and Reconciliation*. Nashville: Abingdon, 1996.

Washington, James M. *The Essential Writings and Speeches of Martin Luther King, Jr.* New York: HarperCollins, 1986.

Watson, Renee. "Five Years After the Levees Broke – Bearing Witness Through Poetry." Accessed August 29, 2018. https://www.rethinkingschools.org/articles/five-years-after-the-levees-broke-bearing-witness-through-poetry.

White, Gillian B. "Searching for the Origins of the Racial Wage Disparity in Jim Crow America." *The Atlantic*. Accessed August 28, 2018. https://www.theatlantic.com/business/archive/2016/02/the-origins-of-the-racial-wage-gap/461892/.

Wilcox, W. Bradford, Wang, Wendy R., and Mincy, Ronald B. "Black men are succeeding in America." Accessed August 28, 2018. http://www.phillytrib.com/news/black-men-are-succeeding-in-america/article_71a67c96-7f07-11e8-a1ce-03d67de5efac.html.

The contents of this monograph were originally presented as a lecture, of the same title, at the Faith at Work Summit (FAWS) in Chicago, IL, October 11-13, 2018. The 2018 Faith at Work Summit, was organized by Trinity Evangelical Divinity School (Deerfield, IL), and brought together a gathering of 500 church and marketplace leaders, desiring to learn from each other and work together to extend Christ's transforming presence into workplaces and industries around the world.

About the Author

Luke Bobo serves as director of resource and curriculum development for Made to Flourish (Overland Park, KS) and works as a visiting professor of contemporary culture and apologetics at Covenant Seminary and of practical theology at Cru's Institute of Biblical Studies. Previously, Luke worked as an electrical engineer. He is the author of *Discipleship With Monday in Mind*, *Living Salty, Light-Filled Lives in the Workplace*, and *A Layperson's Guide to Biblical Interpretation*. Luke currently serves as the minister of Christian education at Friendship Baptist Church in Kansas City, Missouri.